CHRISTMAS CRAC

THE SURVIVOR'S GUIDE

Jokes, stunts, quizzes *and* counter-attack strategies for avoiding the worst and enjoying the best of Christmas!

BUDGIE

CAROLINE PLAISTED

Bloomsbury Children's Books

INCLUDES
MULTIPLE-CHOICE
THANK-YOU
LETTER!

First published in Great Britain in 1995
Bloomsbury Publishing PLC, 2 Soho Square, London W1V 6HB

A CIP catalogue record for this book is available from The British Library

ISBN 0 7475 22537

Illustrations by Woody
Cover and text design by AB3
Printed in Great Britain by
Cox & Wyman Ltd, Reading, Berkshire

10 9 8 7 6 5 4 3 2 1

CHRISTMAS CRACKERED

Caroline Plaisted

Bloomsbury

INTRO

love ya!

So, it's that time of year again. When everything is in Goodwill Overdrive, all yukky, soppy and covered in tinsel. The fridge is full of scrummy food but your mum won't let you eat it – until Christmas Day. Even your family and friends are getting incredibly stroppy about _what_ they ought to buy and for _whom_.

On the other hand, admit it:

THIS YEAR IT IS GOING TO BE AS EXCITING AS EVER...YOU ARE GOING TO GET LOADS OF PRESENTS, GREAT FOOD (EVENTUALLY), AND SEE BRILLIANT TELLY PROGRAMMES...

But stop! You need to make _sure_ you get the best out of Christmas. So don't let the adults swamp your fun, bore you to death, or dominate the telly.

4

MAKE SURE YOU SURVIVE CHRISTMAS,
HAVE A GREAT TIME AND GET ALL THE
CREDIT YOU PROBABLY DON'T DESERVE
FOR BEING THE ACE CHILD OF THE FAMILY!
ALL YOU NEED IS IN THIS BOOK.

So, get cracking on your Christmas strategy
immediately. Have a look at the Contents Page
and decide where you need to start your own
Christmas festivities – and have a great time.

CONTENTS

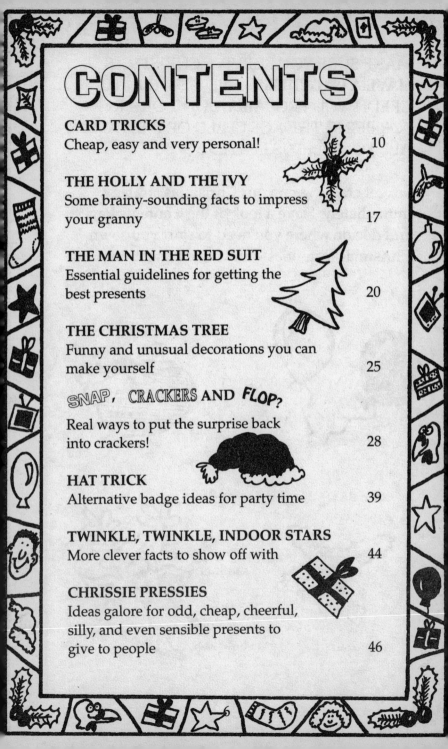

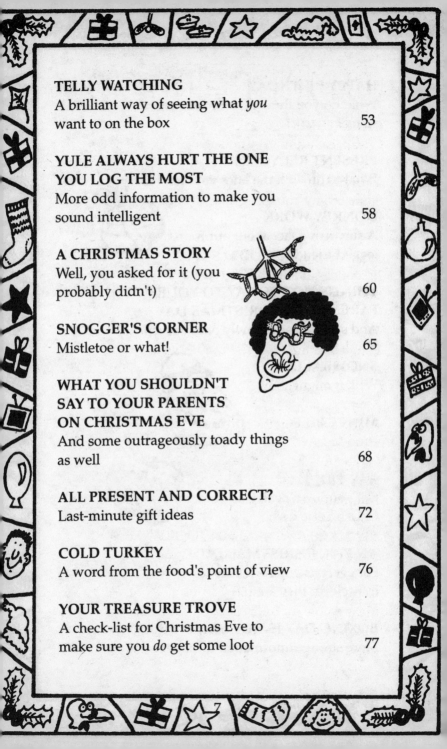

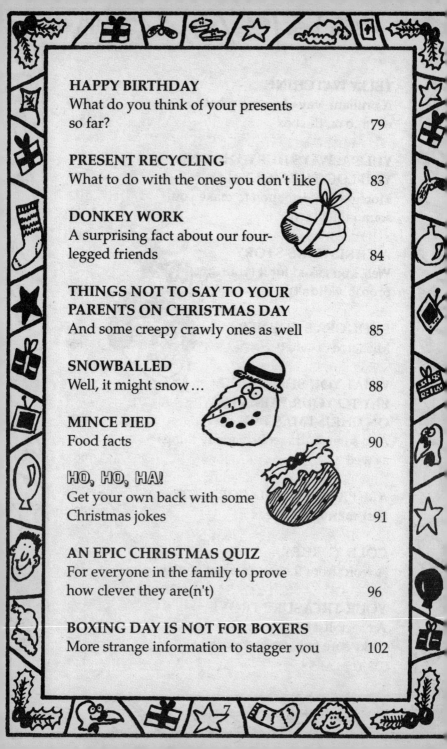

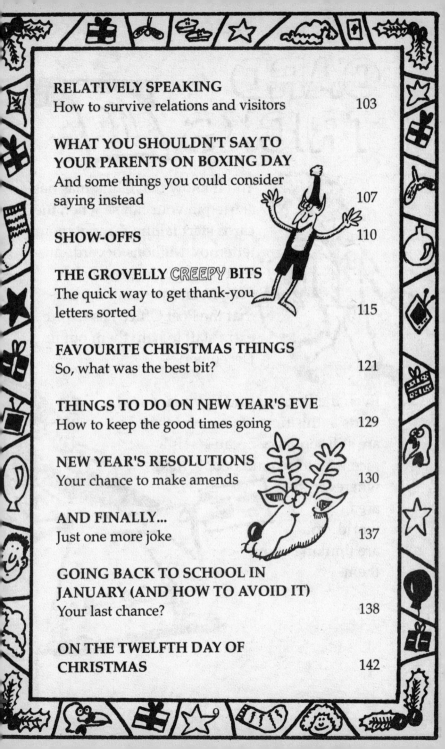

CARD TRICKS

You'll know that Christmas has started in your house when the cards start falling through your letterbox. Millions of cards are sent through the post every year. In fact so many are posted that the Post Office has to hire extra staff to help them out in December!

Even the Romans and Egyptians sent cards at this time of year and they are still sent now because it is a nice way to remind people that, wherever they are in the world, you are thinking about them.

If you haven't yet sent your cards, write down
here all the people you want to send them to:

_____

_____

_____

_____

_____

_____

_____

_____

_____

_____

_____

Now, you could always go out and buy cards but

a) they require lots of money

and

b) you probably haven't got any.

Without doubt, the best thing is to make them
because, even if you have to go out and buy some
paper and envelopes, they'll be much cheaper and,
also, people like grannies and aunties are always
really impressed when they think you have spent
hours making something just for them!

Find some:
paper, pens and pencils, paint,
glittery stuff, envelopes

Fold the paper in half so that it
looks like a card, something like this:

Then draw or paint
a picture on the
front like this:

Then, on the inside, write a message. This could
be done in a rhyme like this:

I want to make a little wish
because you are my Christmas dish!

or this:

I'm tall (and in the hall),
When will the snow fall?

Try making up some rhymes of your own here:

_____

_____

_____

_____

_____

_____

_____

_____

_____

_____

If you really aren't any good at poems, you could always write verses from Christmas carols instead.

Once you've made your own cards, stand back and wait for everyone to go around saying how amazingly talented you are!

(When Christmas is over, don't throw away all the Christmas cards you've been sent. Save them to cut up into gift tags for next Christmas or, better still, find out if the local charity shop is collecting them and give them to a good cause!)

ROBIN REDBREAST

You've probably got millions of ideas about what pictures to draw on your Christmas cards but if you are feeling particularly stupid today, here is an idea. Robins are about the most popular things to appear on Christmas cards ever since the first robin landed on one way back in 1862. The plump little birds are usually seen perched on a Yule log with their scarlet chests glowing. Have you any idea why they have a red chest, though? According to legend, when Jesus was dying on the Cross at Easter, a robin tried to ease His pain by pulling the Crown of Thorns from Jesus' head. As the plucky little robin did this, a drop of His blood plopped on the bird's chest. Which, incidentally, is why it is considered to be good luck if you find a robin's feather.

(By the way, telling your relatives stories like this at Christmas will make them think you are Incredibly Brilliantly Brainy!)

THE HOLLY AND THE IVY

The holly and the ivy,
When they are both full grown,
Of all the trees that are in the wood,
The holly bears the crown:

The rising of the sun
And the running of the deer,
The playing of the merry organ
Sweet singing in the choir.

The holly bears a blossom
As white as the lily flower,
And Mary bore sweet Jesus Christ
To be our sweet Saviour:

The holly bears a prickle
As sharp as any thorn,
And Mary bore sweet Jesus Christ
On Christmas Day in the morn:

The holly bears a bark
As bitter as any gall,
And Mary bore sweet Jesus Christ
For to redeem us all.

The holly and the ivy,
When they are both full grown,
Of all the trees that are in the wood,
The holly bears the crown.

You probably know this song from school but you probably don't know that people used to go to sleep with a piece of holly over their bed so that they got a good night's kip. Some people even used to go as far as picking nine holly leaves at midnight, which they then tied up with nine knots in a handkerchief before popping it under their pillow. This meant they were going to marry but it sounds like a fairly prickly way of going about it.

If you are the person asked to go and get the holly, you'd better be careful. Because a long time ago, if you didn't come home with any, you had your trousers stolen! And worse was to come because the trousers then got nailed to the gate for everyone to see. That way everyone knew they couldn't kiss the owner of the trousers for a whole year! (Perhaps it wasn't so bad after all.)

As far as the ivy in the song is concerned, you could always give some made up into a wreath (a kind of headband) to your dad and grandad because it will stop them from going bald. Ivy's handy for girls too. On January 6th, if a girl holds a piece of ivy to her heart and says this rhyme, she can find herself a husband:

Ivy, ivy, I love you,
In my bosom I put
*   you.*
The first young man
*   who speaks to me,*
My future husband he
*   shall be.*

(There's more about marrying people in SNOGGER'S CORNER if you are interested.)

THE MAN IN THE RED SUIT

Exactly who Father Christmas is is a great mystery. In some countries he is known as Saint Nicholas and all we know about him is that he was a bishop in Turkey. He is still well-known for being a patron saint of children, which is why he only gives presents to children who have been good. (You have been warned!) In some countries, parents tell children that Father Christmas travels around with his friend Black Peter. Without even needing to be told, Father Christmas uses his 'x-ray thought vision' and can tell which children have been good and which ones have been bad. When he gets to the houses where the naughty ones live, he doesn't even go in but sends his friend Black Peter in instead. Rather than leave presents, Pete leaves them a lump of coal. It sounds like bad news (especially if you haven't got a fireplace), so watch out!

Whatever you think of him, can you imagine what Christmas would be like without Santa? Supposing the job as Santa Claus was vacant and you wanted to do it. Do you think you've got the skills required to deliver presents all around the world in a very short time? Why don't you write down what sort of things you think Santa ought to be able to do? We've started the list for you:

Have a long white beard

Be good at reindeer driving

Put your ideas here:

DEAR SANTA...

Saint Nicholas, Father Christmas, Santa –
whatever he's known as in your house and
whether you do or don't believe in him, it's a good
idea to leave him a letter. That way you can make
sure that your parents know what you'd really like
for Christmas. Anyway, it will give them
something to read once you've gone to bed on
Christmas Eve.

This is the sort of thing you could write:

Dear Santa

I really hope that you aren't too exhausted from having whizzed around the world with your reindeer and all that. It is terrific that you had the chance to stop by at our house. Please eat the mince pie and have the drink which I put out for you, otherwise my mum will get fatter and my dad will get really drunk tonight. There is a carrot for the reindeer to nibble on as well. They probably need it to help them see in the dark.

You are quite possibly wondering if I am worthy of some of the many presents you have got on your sleigh. I have, of course, been tremendously well behaved for most of this year — or at least I haven't done any permanent damage to anyone or anything.

What I would really, really, really like for Christmas is

    Everything in the local toy shop
    Loads of sweets
    A shiny new bike
    Some new clothes
    A really good book
    Pens and pencils
    Some CDs
    Some videos
    Money — lots

If there isn't enough space at the foot of my bed, please don't hesitate to leave some of the things (clearly marked with my name) in the living room and/or hallway.

    Have a good trip back to the North Pole.

    With love from

    ME!

(Don't be tempted to put only big and expensive things in your letter; after all, your parents are going to read it and it might put them off giving you anything at all if you do!)

THE CHRISTMAS TREE

You may not know this but the reason why Christmas trees are always evergreens is that they represent everlasting life (EVERgreen – see?). It wasn't until 1847 that people in the United Kingdom started to decorate trees inside the house. The bloke who started it all was Queen Victoria's husband, Prince Albert. He came from Germany where they'd already been Christmas-treeing for centuries.

Choosing the decorations for your own tree is really good fun – especially if everyone in your family gets together to do it. Perhaps you could start buying or making one special decoration each year. Then you can add to your collection every Christmas.

Need some ideas for decorations? How about:

* Milk-bottle tops scrunched together to form balls and cubes (make sure you clean them first or they'll be all pongy after a few days!)

* Baubles made out of old ping-pong balls or golf balls which you've decorated with felt-tip pens

* Crackers (see pages 28–34)

* Sweets (lots of them)

* Brussels sprouts (so that your mum doesn't think you're only interested in sweets!)

* Loo-roll tubes (which you've coloured and

Sweets

Loo-rolls

Old cards

Crackers.

Brussels sprouts

Milk-bottle tops

Paper snowflakes

Pasta shapes

Ping-pong balls

painted)

* Pasta shapes (which you can boil in water with food colouring added)

* Paper snowflakes (like the ones you make at school)

* Old Christmas cards cut up into star shapes (to remind everyone of the stars in the Bethlehem sky)

Go on then – what are you waiting for? Get cracking!

(By the way, have you heard about the more recent Christmas tradition? In 1946, after the end of the Second World War, the people of Oslo, Norway, gave the people of London an enormous Christmas tree for free to thank them for all the help they gave during the war. They continue to do this every year and the tree stands in Trafalgar Square next to Nelson's Column.)

SNAP, CRACKERS AND FLOP?

Sometimes the best thing about crackers is the snap because, after you've dragged someone across the table in an effort to pull the cracker, and retrieved your goodies from the gravy, you'll probably discover that (if your mum has bought cheap crackers) your gift is a rather naff rain bonnet or (of she has bought more expensive ones) a pack of miniature playing cards. Would you be seen out in a bonnet? And do you have miniature hands? The way to achieve a Superior Cracker is to *make your own*.

It doesn't have to be complicated and there are two ways to go about it:

THE FIRST WAY

Buy some cheap crackers and carefully undo them, trying very hard not to damage the outer paper. Take out the present, the motto and the hat but leave the snap where it is. Replace the hat with a badge (see pages 40–43) and the present with a more appropriate one (see pages 47–50) and, if you are especially creative, try writing a new motto (see pages 36–37). (If you prefer you can put in a joke instead, see pages 91–95.)

THE SECOND WAY

If you are the sort of person who makes the things they show you on TV, and who saves Handy Pieces of Cardboard, then you probably know how to make your own crackers already, you Smart Alec. But, just in case you don't, here is how:

1) Rush around the house and find as many cardboard tubes as there are people who need a cracker. You can use kitchen-roll and loo-roll tubes (but make sure they're old ones!) or, especially at this time of year, you can use the long tubes that are left over from wrapping paper and cut them up into shorter tubes. (The longest cracker ever was 45 feet long and had a car inside it – but that might be a bit ambitious to copy!)

2) Now find some paper to form the outside of the cracker. Crêpe paper or wrapping paper is ideal.

3) This is the important bit – the gifts. Find, or buy, things which would be really appropriate or useful to the person you are going to give the cracker to. They obviously have to be small as they need to go in the tube! If you want some ideas, look at this list:

Small things that make good presents:

Sachets of shampoo and bubble bath

Small packets of sweets

Hair nets

Pocket combs

Nail files

Key rings

 Hair ties

Books of stamps

Passport-sized photos of you

Money (highly unlikely!)

Pens and pencils

Small notebooks

Handkerchiefs

Shoe laces

 Earrings

Rings

Paperclips

Bracelets

Cloths to wipe your spectacles with

Packets of sewing needles

Here are some ideas for specific members of your family:

VICTIM	BRILLIANTLY APPROPRIATE GIFT IDEA
Your cousin	Some zit cream for pimply chins
Your sister's boyfriend	One of those sample bottles of breath-freshening mouthwash
Your grandad	A tablet of false-teeth cleaning agent (but make sure you label it in case he pops it in his mouth thinking it's a mint and then gets poisoned!)
Your big sister	An empty sweet packet (because she's always on a diet and you're trying to help her)
Your grandma	One of those money-saving vouchers you always find in magazines
Your mum	One of those cosmetic samples you always find in magazines
Your dad	A feather you found in the park (which he can make into a fishing fly later)

4) Make some badges like the ones on pages 40–43.

5) Write some mottos or jokes (see pages 36–39 and 91–95).

6) Cut a piece of wrapping paper twice as long as the tube and wide enough to wrap itself around the tube one and a half times.

7) Get some paper glue, some bits of tinsel or ribbon and some gift tags.

8) Place a gift, a badge and a motto or joke in each tube.

9) Wrap a piece of the decorative paper around the tube so that it looks just like the sort of crackers you buy in the shops and glue it into position. Pinch the paper on either end of the tube and tie in place with the tinsel or ribbon to stop the contents from falling out.

10) Write the name of the person who will be given the cracker on the gift tag and attach it to the cracker.

11) Now make lots more.

12) Sit back and feel really clever.

(The only problem with making these crackers is they don't have a snap. So, every time someone pulls one of them you must remember to shout 'SNAP!' very loudly!

The reason why crackers have a snap is Mr Thomas Smith, a sweet maker who made the very first cracker, had a shock when one of the logs on his fire exploded with a loud 'snap' one evening. After that he thought it would be staggeringly funny to surprise people with a sweet that cracked or snapped open. Hence the cracker – another fascinating fact to amaze people with.)

MOTTOS

When Thomas Smith made the first cracker, he put in a love message. Over the years, people got a bit embarrassed about some of the soppy verses because you couldn't always be certain that your loved one would read the message (it might end up being given to the old man without any teeth at the end of the table!). So people started to put mottos in crackers instead.

Apart from being very serious, the sort of mottos that come in crackers are often impossible to understand – all that stuff about Confucius and the like. When you ask one of the grown-ups what it really means they usually say something like, 'Don't ask me now, I'm busy' or 'I'm sorry I didn't hear that', because they don't understand either.

Why not try writing your own mottos? Then they could be ones everyone understands and tailor-made for individual people. Here are some to get you started:

A bird in the hand will probably make a terrible mess

Cleanliness takes a lot of time

It never rains except during the summer holidays

Do your homework (but only if you really have to)

An apple a day tastes delicious

Brush your teeth if you want to keep them

Be alert — the country needs lerts

Monday is washing day — but so is every other day of the week

Think of others first — give your children more pocket money

Look after the pennies and it will be ages before they become pounds

You smell!

Your nose is enormous

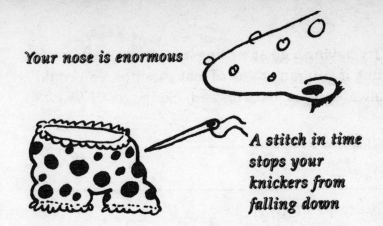

A stitch in time stops your knickers from falling down

Spend, spend, spend (but only other people's money)

Don't forget – a dog isn't just for Christmas. There'll probably be enough left for Boxing Day as well.

Shop early for Christmas – but leave it until Christmas Eve and you'll find some bargains

Christmas isn't just about the telly programmes, you know. It's about all the films as well.

I love you

Be my Valentine even though it isn't February

Don't tell Mum you didn't like the dinner – she made it

Try having a go at writing some mottos yourself. But, if you can't think of many mottos, you could always put in jokes instead. (See pages 91-95.)

_____

_____

_____

_____

_____

_____

_____

_____

_____

_____

_____

HAT TRICK

Of course every year, some bright spark *insists* that you wear the stupid hats that come in crackers. So you all sit around the table in a paper crown that's either far too big or small, feeling, and looking,

like a total Desmond. There's only one way you can get out of it – take the matter into your own hands and introduce the alternative: *badges*.

These are eminently superior to hats because

a) they always fit

and

b) they can bear very appropriate messages.

And all because you can make them! So, rush to the shops now and buy a packet of ready-made, plain-coloured badges. Or, if you are feeling really stingy, get busy with all the safety pins your dad never gets around to throwing away when he picks up the dry cleaning, and an old cornflakes packet. Once you've got the badges you can start being *really* creative with the slogans.

Think of all the things your family do and say

every single Christmas, without fail. For instance, you know how every year your granny always makes you watch the Queen making her speech on telly (when you'd rather be watching the blockbuster film on the other side) and then falls asleep? Well, her badge could say: NOT BORING BUT SNORING.

And you know how your grandad always lets off a nasty smell after the meal? His badge could read: IT WAS THE DOG!

You can probably already think of lots of good ones but here are some suggestions to start you off:

Your mum's badge:
I DON'T EVEN LIKE
BRUSSELS SPROUTS

Your big sister's badge:
I'M A LITTLE CHRISTMAS CRACKER WAITING TO
BE PULLED

Your little sister's badge:
THIS ANIMAL DOESN'T EAT OTHER
ANIMALS

Your dad's badge:
NOT DRUNK, ONLY
RESTING

Your big brother's badge:
DON'T WORRY, YOU CAN BUY ME
ONE NEXT YEAR

For your little brother:
YES – I AM ALWAYS THIS IRRITATING

For your sister's boyfriend:
WELL, SHE THINKS I'M GOOD-LOOKING

For your brother's girlfriend:
MY BUM ISN'T BIG – I'VE JUST
GOT A REALLY SMALL WAIST

For your aunty:
I WAS ALWAYS THE
BRAINY ONE IN THE FAMILY

For your uncle:
I MIGHT MAKE HOME-MADE WINE BUT I NEVER
SAID I DRANK IT

And you don't have to stop at the human
members of your family! You can decorate the
dog's collar or the fish tank as well. How about
these ideas:

For the budgie:
DEFINITELY NOT
A TURKEY

For the cat:
SANTA CLAWS

For the dog:
A DOG IS FOR LIFE
NOT JUST
CHRISTMAS, YOU
KNOW

For the goldfish:
THIS IS NOT A SALMON FARM

For the turkey:
BEST BEFORE 24 DECEMBER
1995

And then of
course you
mustn't
forget your
own badge:
I THINK
MY
PRESENT'S
PROBABLY THE
BIGGEST ONE!

TWINKLE, TWINKLE, INDOOR STARS

One of the good things about it getting dark so early at this time of year is that it's an excuse to put on the Christmas lights. Lots of people don't just put lights on their Christmas trees – they put them all around the window frames and sometimes on the walls as well. A really long time ago (way before there was electricity) people used to light candles to celebrate warmth and the continuance of life (serious stuff, eh?).

You'll also remember that stars and lights led the Wise Men to find Jesus, Mary and Joseph. In Ireland it is traditional for the youngest person in the family to light the

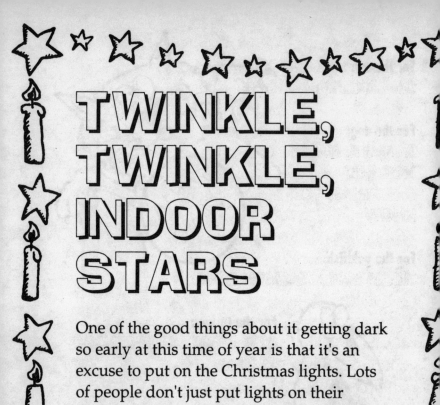

44

Christmas candle on Christmas Eve and to place it in the window to welcome Jesus (and Father Christmas!). In the morning, the oldest person in the family blows the candle out. This does, of course, sound pretty stupid – if you leave a candle burning all night you've got a good chance of burning down the house and all the people and presents with it!

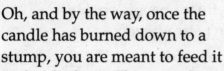

Oh, and by the way, once the candle has burned down to a stump, you are meant to feed it to the chickens. This is said to make them lay well (lay eggs, not go to sleep!) because 'the light of Christmas would shine in them all year long'. That wax must take some chewing.

(This is yet another extremely smart Christmassy thing to impress people with at Christmas dinner.)

CHRISSIE PRESSIES

We all know that being given presents is one of the best things about Christmas but it is also good fun to give them to other people! But choosing what to give can sometimes be really hard. Try to think of things that

    a) You can afford to buy
    b) Will be useful for people's hobbies
    c) They haven't already got

Here are some ideas to get you started:

– *For your mum* –

A book
Something delicious to eat
Your school report (but only if it is a good one!)
A video of her favourite programme
A magazine or newspaper that she enjoys
reading
A picture you've drawn
A photograph of your dad
A promise to wash the car

List your own ideas for presents here:

– *For your dad* –

A book
Something delicious to eat
A photograph of your mum
A story you've written
A painting you've done
A promise to do the hoovering

List your own ideas for presents to give your dad here:

– *For your brothers and sisters* –

Books
A promise of an alibi (for when they get up to
something they shouldn't!)
A poster of their favourite pop star
A scrapbook to keep all their secrets in
A photograph of your mum and dad

List your own ideas for presents to give them here:

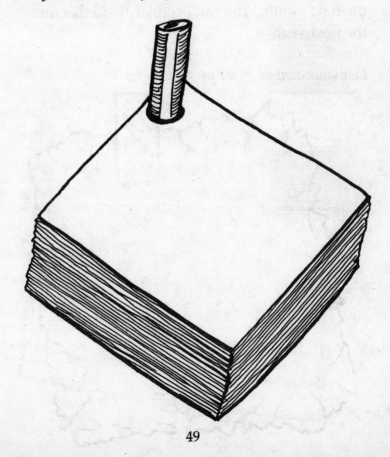

– *Your grandparents* –

A photograph of you
A poem you have written
A book
Your self-portrait
A promise to walk their dog
Six sheets of writing paper and six envelopes
you've addressed to yourself. Tell them you'll
write to them one month and they can write back
the next month. You can promise to do this for
the next year.

List your own ideas for presents here:

Don't forget!

To make sure you don't forget anyone, list all the people you want to (or should!) give presents to here:

Recipient   **Gift idea**

_____   _____

_____   _____

_____   _____

_____   _____

_____   _____

_____   _____

_____   _____

_____   _____

GIFT GIVING

It's traditional to exchange gifts at Christmas time. We do this because it is the way we re-enact the giving of gifts from the Wise Men to Jesus. The Wise Men gave gifts of gold, frankincense and myrrh. If you were a Wise Man, what gift would you give to the baby Jesus if he was born this Christmas?

_____

_____

_____

_____

_____

_____

_____

_____

_____

_____

TELLY WATCHING

This is another major bit of Christmas. There are usually some really good programmes on the box during the festive season, but it can be a problem if you want to watch the Christmas edition of *Gladiators* and your granny wants to watch *The Last of the Summer Wine*. You can:

a) Persuade your parents to buy a second telly.
b) If you've got a video, record the programme you'd rather see and watch it another day.
c) Do your best to make sure that no one knows what is really on the telly.

Points a) and b) probably won't be in your control but c) could very well be. First of all, make sure that you throw away any newspapers that have the Christmas television programmes in them. Second, get hold of the *What's on TV* magazine and work out exactly what you want to watch. Once you've done this, you can't throw the magazine away because that would be too obvious. What you've got to do is  create some programmes of your own and write listings for them which you stick over the ones that you *don't* want someone else to watch.

For instance, if you want to watch *Terminator* and you think your mum will want to watch *Mary Poppins* for the zillionth time, try covering it up with a pretend football match:

2.30pm Football Special

Your chance to see the historic game between the Wimbledon Wombats and the Celtic Carebears which took place in 1991. Featuring dynamic dribbling, fiddly footwork and horrendous hooligans. An absolute must for those with simply nothing else to do.

■ ■ ■ ■ ■ ■ ■ ■ ■ ■ ■ ■ ■ ■ ■ ■ ■

Or you could try writing a spoof film listing:

1.00pm The Grate Escape

Another black and white movie this Christmas. This is the epic story of Cinders who fell out of the fire and got into trouble for burning the hearthrug. Her wicked step-sisters, also known as the Firelighters, are nothing particularly sparkling. OK viewing for people as dynamic as a book of matches.

■ ■ ■ ■ ■ ■ ■ ■ ■ ■ ■ ■ ■ ■ ■ ■ ■

How about this for a comedy programme:

7.00pm The Funny Half-Hour

Totally stupid programme in which a lot of people run around without their trousers on and hide in cupboards. One of the stars is a vicar. Need we say more?

■ ■ ■ ■ ■ ■ ■ ■ ■ ■ ■ ■ ■ ■ ■ ■

This is one for a natural-history programme:

4.00pm The Jungle Book

The original black-and-white version featuring a curious combination of people wearing fake fur suits and others with feathers stuck on their faces and bottoms. This is a silent movie with highly original sub-titles – such as 'Roar'. There is a better movie than this on the other side right now.

■ ■ ■ ■ ■ ■ ■ ■ ■ ■ ■ ■ ■ ■ ■ ■

Want to watch *Michael Barrymore's Christmas Show* and your sister wants to watch the *Brookside* omnibus on the other side? You could try this one:

> **7.00pm Brookside Christmas Omnibus**
>
> Gosh, this makes a change! For the first time in its history, there will not be a murder, a burglary, a crisis for Barry or even an argument in the Close. Instead, all the neighbours will get together for a wine and cheese party. Oops... sorry I yawned...
>
> ■ ■ ■ ■ ■ ■ ■ ■ ■ ■ ■ ■ ■ ■ ■ ■

If you are keen to watch *Home Alone 2,* here is the ultimate one:

> **3.00pm Party Political Broadcast Special**
>
> Special because this out-bores all the party political broadcasting there has ever been. In a unique programme, which will last all evening, every MP is to be given their chance to address the viewers personally. They have ten minutes each – and there are hundreds of MPs, and it's on three channels at the same time! You would be desperate if you wanted to see this. Either that or incredibly dull and boring.
>
> ■ ■ ■ ■ ■ ■ ■ ■ ■ ■ ■ ■ ■ ■ ■ ■

Here are some 'blank' programme listings for you
to fill in. If you need any more, you could copy
the boxes on to some paper:

| 1.00pm | | 3.00pm |

■ ■ ■ ■ ■ ■ ■ ■ ■ ■ ■ ■ ■ ■ ■ ■ ■   ■ ■ ■ ■ ■ ■ ■ ■ ■ ■ ■ ■ ■ ■ ■ ■

| 5.00pm | | 7.00pm |

■ ■ ■ ■ ■ ■ ■ ■ ■ ■ ■ ■ ■ ■ ■ ■ ■   ■ ■ ■ ■ ■ ■ ■ ■ ■ ■ ■ ■ ■ ■ ■

YULE ALWAYS HURT THE ONE YOU LOG THE MOST

If you thought a Yule log was a chocolate Swiss roll covered in icing and sprinkled with icing-

sugar – you are wrong! A Yule log is in fact a ginormous log which is burned on the fire throughout the Christmas holidays to remind people of the warmth of the sun even though it doesn't shine at this time of year. Custom says you should light the log on Christmas Eve from a piece of wood saved from last year's Yule log for luck.

If you want to start a Yule log tradition in your house, why not take your family out for a long country walk to find your own Yule log? Or, if your house hasn't got a fireplace, you might as well stuff your face with a chocolate log – but it probably won't taste very nice if you start off with a bit from last year! Yuck!

(This is another piece of information to stun your mum with.)

A CHRISTMAS STORY

Your creative help is needed! This was going to be a Christmas story but the printing press ran out of print in some of the crucial places. Can you help to complete the story by filling in the gaps?

It was the night before Christmas and everyone was going mad. Mum was stuffing the turkey, my brother was stuffing his face and my dad was out trying to buy some more wrapping paper because we'd run out.

Suddenly, there was a knock at the door! I went to answer it but, at first, I didn't recognise it because I'd never seen a knock before.

'Who's there?' I said.

'Well, it isn't Doctor Who, you moron! Let me in – it's freezing out here,' the Knock said, pushing his way past me and into the hall.

'You'll never believe what happened to me!' the Knock carried on. 'And at Christmas, as well.'

'I won't?' But, before I had the chance to ask, the Knock started to tell me anyway:

Fill in the rest of ⟶
the story here

'I don't believe it! I've never come across a tap-dancing cow in the shopping centre!' I said.

'Are you calling me a fibber?' the Knock shouted.

'Well, no, but exactly which shop did you see her in?'

'The Dairy, of course. But you wait until I tell you about who I met in Boots:

Fill in the rest of the story here ———→

'I think you might be confusing Dick Whittington with Puss-in-Boots,' I told the Knock.

'What's that got to do with anything? The pantomime this year is Jack and the Beanstalk, anyway. Have you got any scoff? I'll have a five-minute egg, please.'

As I was boiling the Knock's egg, there was another knock at the door. When I opened the door, there was another Knock standing there. When I introduced the two Knocks to each other, they started to tell me some Knock, Knock jokes:

Fill in the rest of the story here →

By this time I'd had enough! So I bundled them both up the hall. When we got to the front door, the second Knock suddenly cried out:

Fill in the rest of
the story here

*So what could I do, then? Get a door bell? I needed to
do something drastic, after all, it was nearly time for
supper and:*

Fill in the rest of
the story here

At last the real Christmas celebrations could begin.

The End

SNOGGER'S CORNER

Mistletoe is the stuff with pale green leaves and tiny white berries. It is supposed to have got its name from a legend in which a bird called a mistle thrush accidentally caught a piece of it on its foot before it took off for a quick trip somewhere. Someone spotted the extra 'mistle-toe' on the bird's claw and, when they saw the bird trying hard to shake the foliage off, they laughed so much that they nearly burst their sides. After that, everyone thought that instead of talking about the 'pale green stuff with the white berries' they would start calling it mistletoe.

Now, there is a Christmas tradition about kissing people while standing underneath the mistletoe. This can be a mixed blessing because it is all right to kiss your mum or dad but Uncle Ted's false teeth might be a bit dribbly and as for kissing your brother or sister ... well, would you?

Before everyone starts puckering up on Christmas morning, it might be a good idea to write down here whom you would be prepared to kiss and whom you *wouldn't* want to. That way you can arrange to have an urgent appointment with some washing-up (you'd have to be *really* desperate) or, alternatively, make sure you don't eat any garlic at lunch. Each of the lists has some ideas to get you started:

People I'd like to kiss under the mistletoe

My sweetheart, who is

_____

My dog
My granny
My mum and dad
Mickey Mouse
A millionaire
My favourite pop star, who is

_____

My favourite television star, who is

_____

♡ YES ♡

People I wouldn't like to kiss under the mistletoe

NEVER

NO!

My brother
My sister
My maths teacher
The school caretaker
A donkey
The ugliest person on television, who is

NO!

(By the way, if you are wondering what the tradition of kissing under the mistletoe is all about, here it is: the male kisser has to pick one of the white berries immediately after he's puckered up. When there aren't any berries any more, the kissing is over for this year. Now if you are a girl you *might* consider this to be a problem. This is because it is said that any girl who *is* kissed under the mistletoe is likely to get lots more kisses for the rest of the year BUT any girl who *isn't* kissed is extremely unlikely to get married during the coming year. So, there you have it – the choice is yours!)

WARNING: Whatever you do, don't be tempted to eat (or even kiss) the mistletoe! Not only will it taste yucky, but you won't feel at all well and probably won't last until Christmas Day! YOU HAVE BEEN TOLD!

WHAT YOU SHOULDN'T SAY TO YOUR PARENTS ON CHRISTMAS EVE

'Can't we have Chicken McNuggets?'

You know how irritating it is when you're reading an exciting bit in your book and someone interrupts? Well, that's a bit what it is like for your parents at Christmas. This is because they have A Lot to Organise and Lots of Things on Their Minds. So, in order not to bug your parents too much, here are some it is probably *not* sensible to say on Christmas Eve:

'Should the telly have a blank screen even when it is switched on?'

'I hate turkey.'

'Do we really have to have our cousins for Christmas?'

'I've just seen an advert for a really mega toy on the telly. It's even better than the one I've been telling you about for the last year.'

'Do we have to go to Aunty's house?'

'I don't like
Christmas pudding.'

'Should these Brussels sprouts
have soft bits on them?'

'The cat's just been sick
on the spare bed.'

'Where are we going for
our summer holiday?'

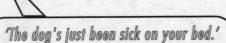

'The dog's just been sick on your bed.'

'My brother's just
sneaked something green and
slimy into his bedroom.'

'Mum, my sister's
getting on my nerves.'

'Do you know what the
budgie's just done all up
the wall?'

OUTGRAGEOUSLY TOADY THINGS TO SAY INSTEAD:

'I think I'll go to bed early tonight.'

'I've just done all the washing-up, peeled all the vegetables and made the stuffing.'

(But don't forget to keep your fingers crossed behind your back, you fibber!)

'Shall I go and watch the telly to get out of your way?'

'Do you want me to do any shopping?'

'You are the best mum and dad in the world!'

(This is a super-toady thing to say on Christmas Eve.)

ALL PRESENT AND CORRECT?

Some people start getting organised for Christmas in January. By July they've bought all their presents and by September everything is already wrapped up and ready for delivery. But it is quite likely that you aren't like that. In fact, it is quite possible that, if you are reading this on Christmas Eve and you *haven't* bought your presents yet, you have *almost* left it too late. This flow chart will help you to work out what to do next:

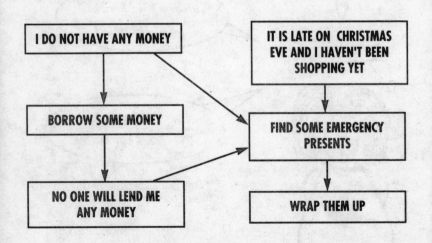

Well, you have left it so late there is no alternative but to find presents from around the house. These will obviously be recycled and the most successfully recycled gifts are those given back to the person they originally belonged to. That way you can be fairly certain that you're giving them something they like! Here are some ideas:

For your mum
Try wrapping up the vegetables that she'll be cooking for Christmas lunch. (If you are a real creep you could peel and prepare them for cooking first.)

For your dad
Donate the telephone directory and tell him that it is unique because it has got his name in it.

For your brother
Give him a broken light bulb and when he realises it doesn't even work, remind him that Real Men aren't afraid of the dark. (He won't dare to complain then!)

For your sister
Find a pair of her knickers and when she asks what you're giving them to her for, remind her that you didn't think she could live without them.

For your granny
You could wrap up her slippers and smile sweetly when she tells you they are just like her most comfortable pair which she mislaid yesterday...

For your grandad
Find the present he gave you last year and give it back to him, telling him that you enjoyed it so much you thought he might like to have a go.

You can probably think of lots of other presents from
around the house. Write your list here:

Recipient   **Perfect gift idea**

_____   _____

_____   _____

_____   _____

_____   _____

_____   _____

_____   _____

_____   _____

_____   _____

_____   _____

_____   _____

COLD TURKEY

Dear Reader

It is a tough life being a turkey — even a free-range one. Of course, in my ancestors' day, being a gobbler wasn't so bad. Until the seventeenth century (I'm a turkey, not a teacher, so don't ask me!), turkeys were running wild in America — but then the Spanish went and took some of my feathered friends to Europe. Next thing we knew, people got a taste for us! In the United Kingdom, folk used to eat roast swan, boar's head and goose — but now more than 10 million of us turkeys have to try dodging Bernard Matthews, Iceland and all those supermarket trolleys every December.

On December 26th I get the chance to relax a little: by then I know that I'm not destined to be dressed in mayonnaise and pickle so I can start planning my winter holiday. What I really like to do is go skiing — those civilised Swiss people seem to prefer cheese and yogurt to turkey sandwiches.

But all too soon it's Easter and there seems to be a fashion for people to eat turkey at this time of year as well. It's enough to ruffle your feathers! So I go to roost for a while.

After Easter I can relax a bit for the next few months. I even went to Barbados for a rest last year. But all that heat was too much — my skin started to crackle! So I came home fast.

Life isn't too bad really until November, when the trouble starts all over again. What can a self-respecting (not self-basting) turkey do to avoid the tin foil?

Yours in sage, rosemary and thyme,

Gobbler

YOUR TREASURE TROVE

Even if you're not sure whether the Man in the Red Suit does distribute the loot, it's a good idea to keep your options open. After all, if he does exist, you might upset Santa if you don't leave out a drink and something to eat for him and the reindeer. And then you might not get any presents at all! Anyway, your parents usually like it if you follow the same traditions every year.

Here's a check-list of things so that you don't forget anything and run the risk of missing out on some of the dosh:

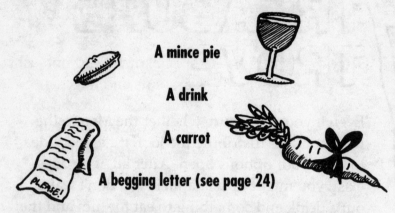

A mince pie

A drink

A carrot

A begging letter (see page 24)

A Christmas stocking (Find out who's got the biggest feet in your family and pinch one of the longest socks they've got!)

A present sack (Think BIG! Forget about a pillow case — find a double duvet cover!)

Make sure you leave everything in the right place before you go to bed. (Don't forget to put the presents you're going to give people under the tree as well!)

HAPPY BIRTHDAY

December 25th is a very special day – and not just because you get loads of presents and the chance to eat as many sweets as you can scoff in one day! Of course, this is the day that we celebrate Jesus' birthday and it is when the Church holds the Mass of Christ. So it's called Christmas – get it?

Mass is usually held at midnight on Christmas Eve and according to folklore, cows and bulls can be found, in their stables and sheds, on their knees and turned towards the East at this time. This is because the cows are bowing in respect of Jesus' birth – just as they did in Bethlehem almost two thousand years ago. (You'll probably remember the carol 'Away in a manger' in which you sing 'The cattle are lowing' - well, that's what that line's all about.)

By the way, if you have a nativity scene as part of the decorations in your house, remember to keep the baby Jesus' manger hidden until last thing on Christmas Eve – otherwise he'll be born too early!

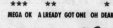

ON CHRISTMAS DAY IN THE MORNING

If you have been really lucky and have received
lots of presents, it might be a good idea to keep a
record of whom gave you what. That way you
won't forget whom to send thank-you letters to!
So, no matter how early it is, grab a pencil.

GIFT	RECEIVED FROM	STAR RATING
_____	_____	_____
_____	_____	_____
_____	_____	_____
_____	_____	_____
_____	_____	_____
_____	_____	_____
_____	_____	_____
_____	_____	_____
_____	_____	_____
_____	_____	_____
_____	_____	_____
_____	_____	_____

***   **   *
MEGA OK   A LREADY GOT ONE   OH DEARr

YOUR BEST CHRISTMAS PRESENTS EVER

Remember the time when someone gave you exactly what you'd been trying to save up for for months? Or when you received an excellent outfit to wear to the next party? Now is your chance to record for posterity, the best presents you've been lucky enough to be given:

FANTASTIC PRESENT   **FANTASTIC-PRESENT GIVER**

_____   _____

_____   _____

_____   _____

_____   _____

_____   _____

_____   _____

_____   _____

_____   _____

_____   _____

_____   _____

_____   _____

_____   _____

THE BEST!

YOUR WORST CHRISTMAS PRESENTS EVER

With luck you'll get really brilliant presents from
Santa this year, but you can probably remember
some fairly Christmas grotto-ones that you've been
given in the past. Like the jumper with three arms,
the pair of slippers with two left feet or the jigsaw
puzzle with two pieces missing. List here all the
presents you wish you'd never had:

GROTTY PRESENT   **GROTTY-PRESENT GIVER**

_____   _____

_____   _____

_____   _____

_____   _____

_____   _____

_____   _____

_____   _____

_____ _____   _____ _____

_____ _____   _____ _____

_____ _____   _____ _____

_____ _____   _____ _____

_____ _____   _____ _____

_____ _____   _____ _____

PRESENT RECYCLING

Even if you've got lots of mega presents, it is more than likely that you'll be given something this year that you don't like or that is exactly the same as something you've already got. The question is – what are you going to do about it?

You could try taking the present back to the shop and either getting the money back (you meany!) or swapping it for something else.

Or how about saving the present and giving it to someone else as a birthday or Christmas present?

But the best thing would be to take the present along to a charity shop and let them sell it to raise much-needed funds. What a nice person you'd be!

DONKEY WORK

What has a donkey got to do with Christmas?
Quite a lot, actually. Remember the long journey
Joseph and Mary made to Bethlehem? Well, they
didn't go on the bus, they went by donkey, didn't
they? If you want proof, go along to your nearest
zoo, donkey sanctuary or farm (there are even
farms in cities these days – ask someone at
the library where the closest one is). Every
single donkey will have a long dark
stripe down its back and another
one across its shoulders,
forming a cross. Amazing,
but true!

THINGS NOT TO SAY TO YOUR PARENTS ON CHRISTMAS DAY

Write your own list of things not to say here:

_____

_____

_____

_____

_____

CREEPY CRAWLY THINGS TO SAY INSTEAD:

SNOWBALLED

Almost everybody loves a white Christmas (the ones with snow, dummy, not the song that Bing Crosby sang!). But did you know that snow is actually made up of small hexagonal ice crystals? A fascinating fact to bore your spotty cousin with is that as the crystals get bigger, they form into flakes and then their weight makes them fall through the air. It's the air trapped between the crystals that makes them sparkle.

In some countries, people say that snow is the result of an old woman plucking a goose in the sky. But now, of course, you know better!

WHAT TO DO IF IT SNOWS:

Make a snowman

Have a snowball fight

Build an igloo

Go sledging

Go skiing

WHAT TO DO IF IT DOESN'T SNOW (or if December is the height of the summer where you live):

Look at a snow-storm paperweight and pretend

Watch *Home Alone* on video

Cut up lots of white loo paper and sprinkle it liberally around the house (then hide from your mother)

MINCE PIED

As you chomp on the next mince pie, you might like to reflect that the first ones were made by the Tudors (you know, people like Henry VIII – the busy one with six wives) all that time ago. The Elizabethans (the ones who lived after Henry died and his daughter Liz became Queen) used to put minced meat, sugar, spices and dried fruit into the pastry cases – yuck! Nowadays, we've stopped putting the meat in but we still have the pastry cases, which are meant to represent the manger that Jesus was laid in, instead of a crib. (The Elizabethans called the pastry cases coffins – but then they liked gory things. They went around chopping people's heads off when they didn't like the look of them!)

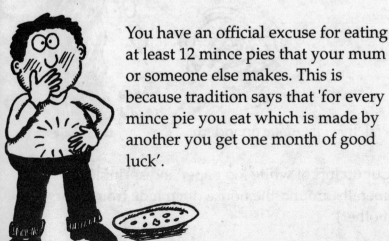

You have an official excuse for eating at least 12 mince pies that your mum or someone else makes. This is because tradition says that 'for every mince pie you eat which is made by another you get one month of good luck'.

HO, HO, HA!

What better way to torture your relatives than to practise all your Christmas jokes on them?

What does Father Christmas call his two cats?
Holly and Ivy

What qualifications did Santa need?
Ho-Ho-Ho-Levels

What qualifications does Santa need now?
GCS-kis

What do you call a priest who only likes Christmas?
Father Christmas, of course!

What is Santa's first name?
The First Noel!

What do you call Santa Claus' wife?
Mary Christmas

What do you call Santa's son?
The Second Noel!

What do you call Santa's daughter?
Christmas Carol

SANTA: Doctor, Doctor, I can't bear being in small places!
DOCTOR: That's because you are suffering from Santaclaustrophobia!

What nationality is Santa Claus?
North Pole-ish

FATHER CHRISTMAS, STUPID!
Father Who?
FATHER
Who's there?
KNOCK, KNOCK!

MARY CHRISTMAS: Santa – have you got holes in your socks?
SANTA: Certainly not!
MARY CHRISTMAS: Well, how did you get them on, then?

SANTA: Mary, it's teeming cats and dogs out there!
MARY CHRISTMAS: Don't be silly – it's only the reindeer.

What does Santa put on his feet?
Christmas stockings

What time was it when Father Christmas met the crocodile? Time for him to run!

What do you call Santa's cat? Santa Claws

Why did Santa send the Head Elf to hospital? Because he had to look after his Elf!

At this time of year, what do you call a really funny joke? A Christmas cracker!

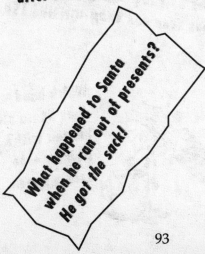

What happened to Santa when he ran out of presents? He got the sack!

What do you call a Father Christmas without underpants? **Saint Knickerless!**

What do you call Father Christmas on Boxing Day? **Exhausted!**

What does Mary Christmas do when it rains?
She gets wet...

Where do the Christmas Gnomes live? **Gnome Sweet Gnome.**

FIRST FRIEND: Have you ever seen a man-eating shark?
SECOND FRIEND: No, but I've seen a man eating turkey.
FIRST FRIEND: Really?
SECOND FRIEND: Yeah — my dad at Christmas.

Which hand does Santa stir his tea with? **Neither — he uses a spoon.**

94

What flour does
Santa's Elves use
to make cakes?
Elf-Raising Flour

Where do you find wild turkeys?
It depends where you left them.

What's white and goes up?
A stupid snowflake.

KNOCK, KNOCK!
Who's there?
WENDY
Wendy Who?
**WENDY RED RED, ROBIN COMES BOB,
BOB, BOBBIN' ALONG...**

What do you get if you
cross a fox with a turkey?
A fox!

AN EPIC CHRISTMAS QUIZ

Yet another good thing
about Christmas is that it
means your whole
family is usually in the
same place at the same time.
This can be a bad thing if your
brother doesn't stop picking his spots or if your big
sister spends the entire time sighing deeply. BUT – it
does mean that you can get the chance to play
games like Monopoly or Mousetrap. The problem is
that you probably played these games last year, and
the year before that, and the year before that, and
the year before that. If you haven't been given a new
game this Christmas (drop heavy hints to your
parents about how deprived your education will be
as a result), this is your chance to hold an EPIC
CHRISTMAS QUIZ.

You can either play as individuals or form two or
more teams of equal size. One person needs to ask
the questions and keep the scores.

And the questions are:

1   Name the presenter of *Telly Addicts*.

2   Who introduced Christmas trees to the United Kingdom?

3   In which country would you find the Great Barrier Reef?

4   Who celebrates their birthday on December 25th?

5   Whom did Juliet fall in love with?

6   Whose bright idea was Red Nose Day?

7   Which group is Tony Mortimer in?

8   Why do cows have sweet breath?

9   Which programme does Pamela Anderson appear in?

10   Which group are David, Damon and Trey in?

11   Which saint is commemorated on December 26th?

12   Who plays Bianca in *EastEnders*?

13   What programme does Chris Rogers present?

14 Whose colours are united?

15 Where are the White Cliffs?

16 What is chocolate made from?

17 What should you do under the mistletoe?

18 What carried Mary to Bethlehem?

19 Who visits naughty children at Christmas?

20 What is the capital of France?

21 Who makes shoes for horses?

22 Who helps Carrie to use Shampoo?

23 What date is Christmas Eve?

24 What is the Queen's surname?

25 What do you eat on Shrove Tuesday?

26 Where do turkeys come from?

27 What has a red breast?

28 What gifts did the Wise Men bring?

29 What *Little* film did Winona Ryder star in this year?

30 Which Christmas book was written by Charles Dickens?

31 Name the presenters on *Blue Peter*.

32 Which county is Newquay in?

33 Which bull likes April and May?

34 Name the bunny with goofy teeth.

35 Patsy and Edina are Absolutely what?

36 What, or who, is Snufkin?

37 What does NSPCC stand for?

38 One of Mozart's first names was Wolfgang. What was the other?

39 What is black and white and read all over?

40 Who is Christopher Dean's partner?

41 Why doesn't *Thunderbird* 4 fly?

42 Who is Barbie's boyfriend?

43 Which large mammal spends all its time in the water?

44 What game is played at Wimbledon?

45 What are Ant and Dec's full names?

46 Where is the White House?

47 What was All Around for Wet Wet Wet?

48 Which teams compete in the University Boat Race each year?

49 Who finds the maze as clear as Crystal?

50 Why should you eat 12 mince pies?

Fifty questions should allow the game to go on long enough for most families. But, if you have a super-brainy one, you may need some more questions. If you do, why not set questions about the dates people in your family have birthdays, what their middle names are (a chance to find out if it is really true that your mum's middle name is Ada!), and what the Top Ten is this Christmas.

WARNING: If the game goes on for too long, you will

a) miss that cartoon on the telly

b) start to get desperate to go to the loo

c) begin to get hungry.

So stop while it's still fun and before everyone starts groaning at you!

ANSWERS

1 Noel Edmonds
2 Prince Albert, Queen Victoria's husband
3 Australia
4 Jesus
5 Romeo
6 Lenny Henry
7 East 17
8 Because it is said that the cow in the stable kept the baby Jesus warm with it's breath and it has been sweet ever since
9 *Baywatch*
10 EYC
11 Saint Stephen
12 Patsy Palmer
13 *Newsround*
14 Benetton
15 Dover
16 Cocoa seeds
17 Have a kiss!
18 A donkey
19 Black Peter
20 Paris
21 A blacksmith
22 Jacquie
23 December 24th
24 Windsor
25 Pancakes
26 America

27 A robin
28 Gold, frankincense and myrrh
29 *Little Women*
30 *A Christmas Carol*
31 Diane-Louise Jordan, Tim Vincent and Stuart Miles
32 Cornwall
33 Taurus
34 Bugs Bunny
35 *Absolutely Fabulous*
36 A friend of Moomin
37 National Society for the Prevention of Cruelty to Children
38 Amadeus
39 A book!
40 Jayne Torvill
41 Because it's a submarine
42 Ken
43 A whale
44 Tennis
45 Ant McPartlin and Declan Donnelly
46 Washington, DC
47 Love
48 Oxford and Cambridge
49 Ed Tudor-Pole
50 Because each pie gives you a month's good luck. 12 pies give you a whole year's worth!

BOXING DAY IS NOT FOR BOXERS!

You might be excused for thinking that this is the day that people like Frank Bruno go on holiday. Actually, it is called Boxing Day because, as long ago as the Roman era, this is the day that money boxes were given to people. The Romans used to give money to athletes to pay to watch them play games but, as time went on, people started to give money to the poor and this was given in alms-boxes.

Why don't you get your family to revive the Boxing Day tradition? Find a suitable box (the bigger the better) and ask everyone in the house to empty their pockets into it. Then ask everyone to nominate a charity that they think the money should go to. If people suggest lots of different ones, select the one that everyone is happy to support. As soon as Christmas is over, hand over the money to the charity you chose.

RELATIVELY SPEAKING

Boxing Day is often the day when either you go to visit your relatives or they come to see you. So you'll probably have to get up quite early and have to look smart. If the people you are going to see gave you one of your Christmas presents, it would be spectacularly creepy if you either wear it (but only if it is an item of clothing) or carry it about all the time you are with them.

With a bit of luck, you will like the people you've got to spend the day with. But if you don't get on very well with them, this could be difficult. You could grin and bear it or, on the other hand, you could try one of the following:

The Highly Contagious Illness

Find a thick red felt pen (but make sure it is not indelible) and paint spots all over your face and neck. After drinking

103

a cup of hot tea, pop a thermometer in your mouth and show it to your mum and dad and whisper, in a croaky voice, that you don't feel very well and that you think you ought to go to bed. If they believe you, they'll cancel the Boxing Day visit and you might, because it is Christmas, get the chance to lie on the sofa watching the telly all day. If they do fall for it, don't forget that you shouldn't laugh too much at the comedy programmes and don't eat too many chocolates!

Burglars

Just before you are due to set off in the car, ask

your parents how common it is for people to be burgled when they are out on Boxing Day leaving the house full of presents. It is quite likely they'll get so worried that they will cancel the trip and you'll be able to spend the day at home.

The Empty Fridge

Hide all the food from the fridge and tell your parents that you saw the neighbour's dog eating the last of it when you got up this morning. Your

parents won't be able to have guests if they can't feed them! (Of course there is a problem with this ploy–if you haven't got any food, what will you eat? How can you replace the food, without letting on what you've been up to? Also, it's just possible that you'll get invited to go to your relatives instead ...)

Survivor's Tips

If there is no alternative to spending time with your relatives, here are some suggestions:

* Don't get into any arguments
* Try not to fight over the telly programmes you want to watch
* Be polite about other people's cooking
* Avoid being sick on their carpet (if you are, you could try blaming it on the dog)
* Smile a lot
* Don't spend hours in the loo
* Read a book

* Try speaking in French all day
  and explain (in French!)
  that you've forgotten
  how to speak English
* Suggest you play a game
* Go out for a walk
* Be nice – it is Christmas,
  after all!

SOME THINGS TO AVOID SAYING

WHAT YOU SHOULDN'T SAY TO YOUR PARENTS ON BOXING DAY

'Did you keep the receipt?'

'The batteries have run out.'

'I hate turkey.'

'When can I take it back?'

'There's smoke coming out of the back of the telly.'

Write your own list of things here:

CREEPY THINGS YOU COULD CONSIDER SAYING INSTEAD:

SHOW-OFFS

You've eaten the hot turkey and now you've eaten it cold with salad. The presents have been opened and the best films were on last night (after you were told to go to bed, of course). Today is Boxing Day and what are you going to do to survive an entire day with your nosey aunt and your dead boring, dopey cousin? Well, with a bit of luck, everyone will still be in a good mood – it's called Christmas cheer (even if you might be tempted to think that the adults have been at the Christmas spirits...).

Now, once upon a time, in ancient history, whenever their relatives came to visit, people like your great-great-grandparents were expected to do a party piece. (Party piece is an old-fashioned word for showing off.) Their party piece would be reading a poem, or playing a piece of piano music, or performing a dance. How embarrassing!

It's a great relief to know that, unless someone like your Great-Aunty Mabel is coming for tea, you won't be expected to perform in front of anyone. (It's an even greater relief to know that you won't have to listen to your snotty cousin scratching his way through a violin concerto … If he's brought his violin with him, go and hide it in the garage quickly!) But everyone likes to show off and that includes your mum and dad.

Why not have a family talent competition? Your granny could do her impression of Hyacinth Bucket and your grandad could do his one of Victor Meldrew (bad luck if they don't have to pretend to be like them!). Your mum could whine along to the last Eurovision song or do her version of Pauline Fowler on *EastEnders*. What about your dad? If you've heard his impression of Meatloaf while he's in the shower, you might be better off encouraging him to whistle like the milkman!

Here are some ideas for party pieces which could be done by anyone in your family:

Postman Pat (everyone knows the words to the song!)

A Power Ranger

The lead singer of the number-one group in the charts

The cat on the roof in *Coronation Street*

A tractor in *Emmerdale*

Your next-door neighbour putting out the dustbins

A chicken (tuck your thumbs under your armpits and 'peck' around the room going *Cluck cluck* before you plonk yourself in the corner, screech and pretend to lay an egg!)

A blade of grass (stand quite still with your arms at your sides)

Bugs Bunny (What's up, Doc?)

A radio show (you'll need to get a tape recorder ready with about three songs – any more and you could get boring!)

Your dad when he's asleep (lie on the sofa and snore loudly)

Frank Bruno

Your granny when she's doing her aerobics

A teapot (put one hand on your hip and stick the other arm out, slightly bent, at the side)

A bird (flap your arms at your side and say *tweet tweet*)

Paula Yates doing *The Big Breakfast* interview with your cat

Sumo wrestling (watch out for your mum's ornaments)

Of course, you could always play a piano concerto, recite a rhyme in fluent French and dance on your toes, but you *are* meant to be enjoying yourself!

Before everyone does their turn, give each member of the family a pencil and a piece of paper. After each act, everyone should award the performer marks out of ten. DON'T tell everyone what the scores are – write them down secretly. At the end of the show, ask the brainiest person at maths to count up the marks. You've probably guessed that the person with the highest score is the winner.

And the prize? That's up to you but here are some suggestions:

Breakfast in bed the next morning
A round of applause
A box of chocolates
An escape from doing the washing-up
A million pounds (donated from the Monopoly set)

THE GROVELLY CREEPY BITS

The worst thing about receiving presents is that your parents expect you to write back and say 'thank you'. They'll probably start nagging you about it the day after Boxing Day.

It is very tempting to be lazy, stuff another box of chocs down your throat and watch a film on the telly. But you've got to think ahead. If you don't say thank you for the presents you got this year, the people who gave them to you *might not buy you a present next year*. In fact, some people might stop buying you birthday presents as well.

So think of the time it takes you to write them as an investment. Anyway, it won't take you too long to write a few really toady lines to people. But, if you are stuck in a post-Christmas permanent pause and can't get your creative writing skills going, you could always use the following ideas. These are so quick and easy that all you have to do is tick the appropriate boxes and sign your name.

So start thanking people now!

Dear Granny

Thank you for the

- ☐ lovely
- ☐ unusual
- ☐ extraordinary

present that you gave me for Christmas. I have

- ☐ never had one before.
- ☐ two already.
- ☐ never seen anything quite like it.

It must have taken you ages to

- ☐ make it.
- ☐ find one in the shops.
- ☐ wrap up such an unusual shape.

I shall

- ☐ treasure it for ever.
- ☐ find a special place to keep it in the cupboard.
- ☐ share it with my brothers and sisters.

I do hope that you

- ☐ find your teeth
- ☐ get less grumpy
- ☐ win the Lottery

in the New Year.

With love from

Dear Mum and Dad

Thank you so much for the incredibly generous present you gave me for Christmas. What a lucky child I am to have parents like you! Your gift was

☐ exactly what I'd been dropping hints about all year.
☐ slightly smaller than the one I saw in the shops but quite possibly nicer.
☐ not at all what I was expecting.

It was

☐ a shame you didn't remember to buy any batteries.
☐ a good thing it was so noisy it drove Aunty Nellie home early.
☐ so thoughtful of you to buy something for all the family to share.

Now that we have almost come to the end of the year, the time has come to

☐ think about my birthday present.
☐ review my pocket money.
☐ buy another telly.

We must hold a family conference about it soon.

Thank you again for giving all of us such a really special Christmas.

With love from your devoted child.

Dear Mean Person

Isn't it incredible that Christmas-present time has been and gone again? Although I expect it is because

☐ you are so incredibly busy earning pots of money
☐ have so many people to buy presents for
☐ normally buy gifts for birthdays

that you forgot to give me my present again this year.

Please do not

☐ feel guilty about this.
☐ worry that I was upset, as I will get over it.
☐ think you can get off lightly.

Of course, you could always consider

☐ buying me something in the sales.
☐ giving me money instead.
☐ being unbelievably nice to me for the next 12 months.

With every good wish for the New Year,

Dear Aunty and Uncle

It was extra-special that you could be with us for the Christmas holiday this year. Especially because

- ☐ *it meant you bought me a better present.*
- ☐ *your cooking is better than ours.*
- ☐ *I had to give up my bedroom for you.*

You are both very talented at

- ☐ *recycling last year's presents to you.*
- ☐ *cleaning up fire-damaged stock.*
- ☐ *finding such unique presents.*

It was so fortunate that the present you so kindly gave me was

- ☐ *not what I gave you last time.*
- ☐ *still able to work.*
- ☐ *small enough to fit in my pocket.*

I shall

- ☐ *do my best to translate the Chinese instructions.*
- ☐ *find the unusual battery that fits it.*
- ☐ *look after it so that you can borrow it from me.*

With every good wish for your safe journey home,

Of course, it isn't always appropriate to send humorous letters to people. So you might find the following letter simple enough to adapt to send to most people:

Dear _____

Thank you very much for the really nice _____ that you kindly sent me for Christmas. It was just what I wanted.

I do hope you enjoyed Christmas as much as I did.

With love from

FAVOURITE CHRISTMAS THINGS

Now that you've stuffed yourself with so much food you feel like a turkey, your eyeballs are glazed with all the telly and your relatives have gone home again for another year, the time has come to reflect on all the really good things that have happened this Christmas.

MY FAVOURITE PEOPLE THIS CHRISTMAS WERE:

_____

_____

_____

_____

_____

_____

_____

_____

_____

_____

_____

_____

_____

_____

THE DELICIOUS FOOD I ATE WAS:

_____

_____

_____

_____

_____

_____

_____

_____

_____

_____

_____

_____

_____

MY FAVOURITE CHRISTMAS SONGS AND CAROLS WERE:

_____

_____

_____

_____

_____

_____

_____

_____

_____

_____

_____

_____

_____

_____

_____

_____

_____

THE BEST PROGRAMMES I SAW WERE:

_____

_____

_____

_____

_____

_____

_____

_____

_____

_____

_____

_____

_____

_____

_____

_____

_____

_____

THE MOST BRILLIANT BOOKS I READ WERE:

_____

_____

_____

_____

_____

_____

_____

_____

_____

_____

_____

_____

_____

_____

_____

_____

THE REALLY EXCELLENT GAMES I PLAYED WERE:

_____
_____
_____
_____
_____
_____
_____
_____
_____
_____
_____
_____
_____
_____
_____

THE PARTIES I WENT TO WERE GIVEN BY:

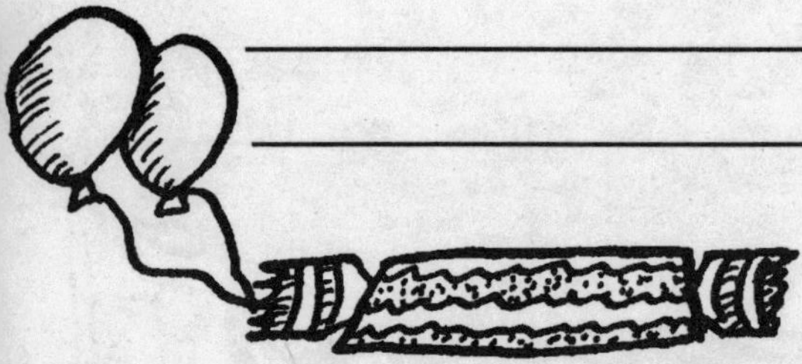

_____

_____

_____

_____

_____

_____

_____

_____

_____

_____

_____

_____

_____

_____

_____

_____

THINGS TO DO ON NEW YEAR'S EVE

You mean that even with all those new things you got for Christmas you still can't think of anything to do? Here are some suggestions for the last day of the year:

Fill in all the list of your favourite things this Christmas (see pages 122–28)

Tidy your room (if you are really desperate!)

Write your New Year's resolutions (see pages 132–33)

Visit a friend (but don't forget to ask your parents' permission first!)

Go with someone to the sales

Get your diary sorted for the New Year (if you haven't already bought a diary, go out and buy one, or better still make one, now!)

Pack your satchel ready for the new term (you total creep!)

Help to organise a New Year's Eve party

NEW YEAR'S RESOLUTIONS

So Christmas has been and gone and there is probably still at least a week before it's time to go back to school. The New Year is around the corner – but the question is, are you ready for it? What is there to be ready for? you might ask yourself. Well, you remember all those things you did in the previous year that you wish you hadn't? Like rowing with your brothers and sisters and always leaving your weekend homework until late on Sunday night? Or how about all those things that you wish you *had* done last year? Like taking the dog for more walks or visiting the old lady who lives across the road more often?

The New Year is a great time for planning and starting afresh. You can resolve to do some things differently in the coming year – that's why they are called New Year's resolutions!

So what New Year's resolutions are you going to make? (You could have two lists of resolutions: one list which your parents would be pleased with and another list which you might want to keep secret!) Here is a list someone wrote last year which you might like to read:

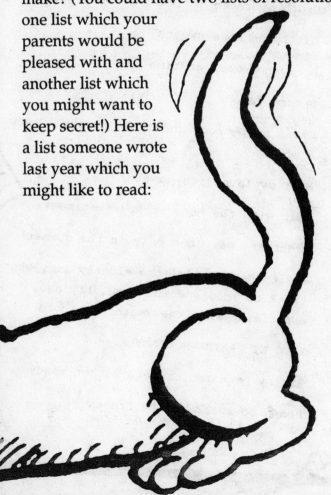

IN THE NEW YEAR I RESOLVE TO:

Brush my teeth at least twice a day

Eat loads more sweets

Do my homework on time

Become famous

Clean my bedroom regularly (probably once a month)

Meet my favourite popstar

Help with the housework (sometimes)

Clean the car (but only in the summer)

Visit Mrs O'Grady (the elderly lady who lives two doors down) regularly and especially when the weather is cold

EDOC NI YRAID YM ETIRW*

Ask my parents for more pocket money

Learn to speak fluent French

Get my own back on my maths teacher

Watch less television after 10.30pm

Watch more telly after school

Go out for long walks with our dog

Avoid walking my dog in puddles so that I don't have to give him a bath when we get home

Help with the washing-up (but only if my brothers and sisters do too!)

Read two new books each month

Write a bestselling book which will earn me loads of pocket money

Go to bed on time (during the week anyway)

Pass all my exams at school

Have everything ready for Christmas by the end of November

Learn how to make a chocolate cake

(*Write my diary in code-dumbo!)

Phew! It is a pretty long list and you can see how the person who wrote it felt full of good intentions and ideas – what a smug creep! Why don't you have a go at writing down your New Year's resolutions here?

TOP SECRET

My New Year's resolutions:

I wrote these on:

Signed:

Do you think you'll be able to keep any of your resolutions? Have a look at your list at the end of January to see how well you are doing and if you've already broken any of them.

My January review of my New Year's resolutions:

RESOLUTIONS I HAVE KEPT

_____

_____

_____

_____

_____

_____

_____

_____

_____

_____

RESOLUTIONS I HAVE BROKEN

_____

_____

_____

_____

_____

_____

_____

_____

_____

_____

Signed:

Date:

Depending on how organised you are, you could also look at this list in June and see how well you got on. Maybe you could even review the resolutions in December as well!

AND FINALLY...

QUESTION:
What did the turkey say on New Year's Day?

ANSWER:
Phew!

GOING BACK TO SCHOOL IN JANUARY (AND HOW TO AVOID IT)

After all the excitement of Christmas and New Year, going back to school will probably seem like a bit of a let-down. The good things about it are that you'll see lots of your mates you haven't seen since the end of term and you can find out about all the things they got up to at Christmas and swop notes about all the brilliant presents you got. You will also get the chance to be away from your brothers and sisters for a while. But, if you really don't want to go back to school, you could always find an excuse to help you avoid it. The question is what and how? Read on:

EXCUSE NUMBER ONE: The inexplicable loss of voice

If you are a chatterbox you may find this the hardest to do but if you can do it, it will probably be the most successful ploy. What you do is keep absolutely silent, starting from the evening before you go back to school. Don't utter a squeak – not even if a mouse runs up your trouser leg! For extra dramatic effect, pretend to try having a conversation with your mum and dad and wave your arms up and down and point to your mouth. This will get them worried and you'll avoid at least the first day at school, although you will have to be prepared to be taken to the doctor.

EXCUSE NUMBER TWO: The letter from the headteacher

Copy this note in your neatest handwriting:

Dear Parents

Owing to a problem with the central heating boiler, the start of the new school term will be delayed by at least one week. As all students studied so hard last term there is no need for them to do any homework and studying instead of being at school this week. Let them watch television, relax as much as possible and go to bed late every night for the next week.

Yours sincerely,

Headteacher

Can you think of any other excuses? Or have you any others that you've used in the past? Write them down here:

ON THE TWELFTH DAY OF CHRISTMAS

You must have sung the song called 'The Twelve Days of Christmas'. You know, the one about pear trees, rings and French hens? Once upon a time, a really long time ago–even before your parents were born–Christmas lasted for 12 days! Can you imagine that?

Now people usually finish the Christmas festivities soon after Boxing Day, although they leave the Christmas decorations up till 6th January, or Twelfth Night as it is called. This day is also known as the Feast of Epiphany (how many names does one day need?) which marks the official end of Christmas.

It was allegedly on this day that the Wise Men arrived at the now famous stable in Bethlehem. So this is the real end of Christmas and you absolutely have to take down every single Christmas decoration or you could suffer from all sorts of bad luck! Now you might feel a bit sad about having the house look so bare after all the sparkles of Christmas but there is one good thing about all of this: the decorations don't have to be taken down until midnight. You could always tell your mum and dad that you ought to stay up late to help them. Well, it's worth a try!